Liveson Tatira

The Shona Culture

Liveson Tatira

The Shona Culture

The Shona People's Culture

LAP LAMBERT Academic Publishing

Impressum/Imprint (nur für Deutschland/ only for Germany)
Bibliografische Information der Deutschen Nationalbibliothek: Die Deutsche Nationalbibliothek
verzeichnet diese Publikation in der Deutschen Nationalbibliografie; detaillierte bibliografische
Daten sind im Internet über http://dnb.d-nb.de abrufbar.
 Alle in diesem Buch genannten Marken und Produktnamen unterliegen warenzeichen-, marken-
oder patentrechtlichem Schutz bzw. sind Warenzeichen oder eingetragene Warenzeichen der
jeweiligen Inhaber. Die Wiedergabe von Marken, Produktnamen, Gebrauchsnamen,
Handelsnamen, Warenbezeichnungen u.s.w. in diesem Werk berechtigt auch ohne besondere
Kennzeichnung nicht zu der Annahme, dass solche Namen im Sinne der Warenzeichen- und
Markenschutzgesetzgebung als frei zu betrachten wären und daher von jedermann benutzt
werden dürften.

Coverbild: www.ingimage.com

Verlag: LAP LAMBERT Academic Publishing GmbH & Co. KG
Dudweiler Landstr. 99, 66123 Saarbrücken, Deutschland
Telefon +49 681 3720-310, Telefax +49 681 3720-3109
Email: info@lap-publishing.com

Herstellung in Deutschland:
Schaltungsdienst Lange o.H.G., Berlin
Books on Demand GmbH, Norderstedt
Reha GmbH, Saarbrücken
Amazon Distribution GmbH, Leipzig
ISBN: 978-3-8433-8643-2

Imprint (only for USA, GB)
Bibliographic information published by the Deutsche Nationalbibliothek: The Deutsche
Nationalbibliothek lists this publication in the Deutsche Nationalbibliografie; detailed
bibliographic data are available in the Internet at http://dnb.d-nb.de.
 Any brand names and product names mentioned in this book are subject to trademark, brand
or patent protection and are trademarks or registered trademarks of their respective holders.
The use of brand names, product names, common names, trade names, product descriptions
etc. even without a particular marking in this works is in no way to be construed to mean that
such names may be regarded as unrestricted in respect of trademark and brand protection
legislation and could thus be used by anyone.

Cover image: www.ingimage.com

Publisher: LAP LAMBERT Academic Publishing GmbH & Co. KG
Dudweiler Landstr. 99, 66123 Saarbrücken, Germany
Phone +49 681 3720-310, Fax +49 681 3720-3109
Email: info@lap-publishing.com

Printed in the U.S.A.
Printed in the U.K. by (see last page)
ISBN: 978-3-8433-8643-2

Waterstones

1 Priorsgate
Warwick Street
Leamington Spa
CV32 4QG
01926 883804

SALE TRANSACTION

SHONA CULTURE, THE	£42.00
9783843386432	
Clearance	**-£39.00**

No. items 1
Balance to pay

£3.00

Cash £3.00

- - - - - - - - - - - - - - - - - -

WATERSTONES REWARDS POINTS
WATERSTONES REWARDS POINTS WOULD HAVE
EARNED YOU 9 POINTS TODAY
ON ITEMS WORTH £3.00
Apply now at thewaterstonescard.com

- - - - - - - - - - - - - - - - - -

VAT Reg No. GB 108 2770 24

STORE	TILL	OP NO.	TRANS.	DATE	TIME
0170	3	815713	218314	17/07/2017	16:15

9990201700032183144

Waterstones

Refunds & exchanges

We will happily refund or exchange
goods within 30 days or at the manager's
discretion. Please bring them back with
this receipt and in resalable condition.
There are some exclusions such as Book
Tokens and specially ordered items, so
please ask a bookseller for details.

This does not affect your statutory rights.

Waterstones Booksellers,
203/206 Piccadilly, London, W1J 9HD.

Get in touch with us:
customerservice@waterstones.com
or 0808 118 8787.

Buy online at Waterstones.com or Click & Collect.
Reserve online. Collect at your local bookshop.

Did you love the last book you read? Share your
thoughts by reviewing on Waterstones.com

Waterstones

Refunds & exchanges

We will happily refund or exchange
goods within 30 days or at the manager's
discretion. Please bring them back with
this receipt and in resalable condition.
There are some exclusions such as Book
Tokens and specially ordered items, so
please ask a bookseller for details.

This does not affect your statutory rights.

Waterstones Booksellers,
203/206 Piccadilly, London, W1J 9HD.

Get in touch with us:
customerservice@waterstones.com
or 0808 118 8787.

Buy online at Waterstones.com or Click & Collect.

Shona Culture

Table of Contents 2

3

Dedication

This book is dedicated to my beloved dear wife Shamiso Tatira. She has been a treasure in my life as way back as when we were just but humble pupils at Gutu High School up to this time of the publication of my third book. It has been a long life of supporting each other. Your unfailing support, maturity, intellectual dexterity and affection which are abundantly evident in you when it comes to dealing with matters of life are forever highly cherished. *NDINOKUVONGAI VACHIHERA*. May our faithful God continues to bless you abundantly.

Acknowledgements

A book of this nature cannot be written in a vacuum both physical and social. For this reason, the author would, therefore, like to extend his deepest gratitude to the following:

My most beloved late parents, Mr Ephraim, Ndoroyashe, Chifeke, Tatira and Mrs Chiedza, Tambudzai, Chifeke, Tatira for their entire life they devoted to me and my five brothers. They made us people with names and reputation. Gave us a religion – Christianity to follow and above all led an exemplary life which we followed with pride. Hard working and unquestionable integrity are the virtues which they never tired to teach and enforce. *Ndinovonga hangu.*

My beloved brothers Mr Herbert Tatira and his family and Rev. Dr. Simbarashe, Gutu, Tatira and his family. The two giants have kept our families focused and united. They have and continue to be my pillars of strength. May the Lord continues to bless you and your families. *Zvirambe zvakadero vanamukoma naanamaiguru nevafana.* Your support has enabled yet again the publication of my third book.

My beloved sons, Herbert and Cephas for all their support and encouragement they offered me during the lonely journey of writing this volume. Remain focused and you will achieve whatever ambitions you have in life.

Dr Francis, Matambirofa, indeed my brother, for all the support which he gave me when I was writing this book. Your unfailing support is very much appreciated and may you continue to assist as you have always been doing. *Zvinovongwa Mutadza!!*

However, the finishing of this book would not have been possible without the unfailing support of my most beloved wife, Shamiso. I would like to express special thanks to her for always being there for me. Writing is a lone activity which demands a wife whose support and encouragement are unquestionable, Shamiso proved exceptionally a perfect match for such an activity. She constantly asked me about the progress of the book. Thank you very much for the love and support. May the dear Lord continues to abundantly bless you. *Ndizvozvo vaChihera, vaNyachide!!!!.*

Foreword

This book explores Shona culture and begins by tracing the origin of the Shona people. The Shona people are a group of people who are considered to be part of a larger group of the Bantu people of Africa. There are two contrasting views about the movement of the Shona from Northern Africa to Southern Africa. Interestingly, both views are agreed that the Shona people moved from the north to the south. The book covers topics on the Shona family, marriage, traditional beliefs and the rites of passage. These are considered to be of phenomenal importance when we talk about Shona culture. The book explores the Shona family, their way of getting married, their beliefs and their rites of passage in the hope that readers would discover that, the Shona people's culture is fundamentally different from how the western people view it. There is a need to understand the Shona culture from an Afro-centric perspective rather than to critique it from outside. Critiquing it from outside brings in the danger of condemning almost everything about the Shona culture. In this book, all the beliefs are rationalised using the Afro-centric approach. The book also argues that the Shona are monotheist when it comes to religion. It puts to rest the debate that considered the Shona as people who are animistic. The Shona people believe in one God whom they have various names for. They have other beliefs like witchcraft and avenging spirits. The book also explores the foreign influence as far as it has impacted on the Shona belief system. The influence has been both negative and positive. There are some beliefs which have stood the test of time while others have been modified, and yet others have completely given way to the foreign influence.

Chapter 1

The Shona family

1.1 Introduction

Before we talk about the Shona family, we should know who these Shona people are. The Shona people like any other people, have their own history. In this introduction we shall attempt to locate the origin of the Shona people as well as the origin of the name Shona.

1.2 Historical background of the Shona people

The Shona people are part of a larger group of people called the Bantu people. The word Bantu referred to people of dark skin, with flat noses who had a common root *ntu* in various forms for human being. The name for a human being in different Bantu languages is as follows:

Shona   mu-nhu

Zulu   umu-ntu

Sotho   mo-tho

Chewa   mu-ntu

Venda   mu-nhu

Seligman, C.G. (1966:117) writing about the Bantu people notes,

> The Bantu are congeries of peoples belonging predominantly to Central

and Southern Africa, named from and defined by the familiar type of
language that they speak, which is generally considered to have originated in
the neighbourhood of Great Lakes.

Seligman (1966) argues that some of the Bantu people are now found in the region he
calls Southern Bantu which includes areas of Zimbabwe, parts of Mozambique, South
Africa, Swaziland, Namibia, Botswana and Lesotho. In support of the same view, Nzita,
R and Niwampa, M (1993:6) observe,

The Bantu are said to have originated from somewhere in the Congo region
of Central Africa and spread rapidly to the Southern and Eastern Africa.

Mutswairo, S (1996:6) postitulates that the Shona, preferring the term Mbire, migrated
from the North at some time between 300 and 200 BC and by 500-300AD the people had
reached the sub region as further down as Eastern Cape.

To back the argument that the present Shona people originated from the North and
moved Southwards, Mutswairo postulates a hypothesis, which he calls the Mbire
Hypothesis.

1.2.1 Mbire Hypothesis

Mutswairo (1996) advances a hypothesis which he calls Mbire hypothesis. He argues
that the Mbire (current Shona people) were part of the Bantu migration. Using oral
tradition he collected from Shona elders, Mutswairo postulates that the Mbire, now
Shona but then Nduwi migrated from the North, in Ethiopia and moved Southwards
and temporarily settled in Tanzania. They moved Southwards as an integral part of the
Nduwi.

It is when they arrived in Tanzania that one group rebelled. The rebellious group was
named monkey, baboon and they assumed the totem Soko. From this incident, the
group was known as VaMbire, taking their name after their leader Mambire (Mambiro).
These people named the place Guruuswa, meaning the place of tall grasses. The group

which rebelled was left behind by a group which was led by Maumbe. The group is that of the Dziva-Hungwe people.

The Mbire-Soko followed after some time only to find the Dziva people already in Zimbabwe. Chigwedere does not believe that the Mbire and Dziva were once an integral group, but takes them to be different groups who migrated independently of each other (Chigwedere, 1980). Though Mutswairo and Chigwedere do not agree on how these people moved from the North to the South, they are agreed on the fact that the Shona, then Nduwi/Mbire people moved from the North to the South.

In their movement, they broke in separate groups whenever leadership crisis occurred. Some leaders died on the way because of war and natural disasters. The leaders of the Mbire group who crossed the Zambezi River are said to have been under the leadership of Chaminuka's sons. Mutswairo notes,

> When the ancestor fathers: Mambiri, Tovela(Tovera), Murenga, Runje,
>
> Chaminuka, Mushavatu and Nehanda had perished, the Mbire journed
>
> South and crossed the Zambezi River under the leadership of Chaminuka's sons,
>
> Kutamadzoka, Chigwango and Kauswere. This was around 100AD.

Probably readers might be asking questions as to why all these movements. Reasons for these movements can only be speculated as follows:

a) The Bantu might have been searching for bigger pastures for their animals,

b) The Bantu might have been moving away from the encroaching Sahara Desert,

c) Because of lack of geo-political boundaries, people could have migrated for sheer adventure,

e) They might have been fleeing from the militant Moslems who wanted to make Bantu believe Muslim religion as it is known that around 639-643AD, Moslem militants attacked the Northern countries namely Sudan and Egypt with the aim of converting these territories into Muslim territories (Mutswairo 1996).

Whatever reasons that can be given, it should be noted that there was a legitimate reason for such migration. Large groups of people as evidenced by this migration cannot just happen without a legitimate cause. We have seen that the Bantu people migrated to the South and among these were the Mbire people, therefore we would like to investigate how these Mbire people became to be known as the Shona people.

1.2.2 Origin of the name Shona

Both the European and African scholars agree that the name Shona is not an indigenous name for the Zimbabwean people. This is true because in Zimbabwe there is no single group of Shona people that has the name SHONA as their clan name neither is there anyone with a Chidawo(praise name) SHONA. Among all the chiefs in Zimbabwe, there is no single chief called chief SHONA.

Different scholars have their own views about the origin of the name Shona. Beach(1980:18) explains,

> The word itself was apparently first used by the Ndebele and others
>
> to the South in the early 19th century to describe the people of South-West of the Plateau, especially the Rozvi. The word extended by degrees first to the Central Shona and then to the rest of the Shona people.

Theal in Mutswairo (1996:34) notes,

> The word Mashona is contemptuous nickname given
>
> by enemies and adopted by us (Whites) unwittingly, but it is
>
> now in general use by Europeans.

Mutswairo also believes that the name is of foreign origin. He believes that the name came in use during the Ndebele raids of the Rozvi in the 19th century. The Rozvi people used to flee from the marauding Ndebele warriors. The name Shona was derived from the Zulu word ukushona which means to flee or disappear (Mutswairo, 1996).

Therefore, it can be seen that all the scholars agree that the name Shona is of foreign origin and was used as a derogatory term to describe the original inhabitants of this country. It is Doke, who legitimised that name. Doke a linguist from South Africa, adopted the name to label all the people who spoke dialects which were mutually intelligible namely Karanga, Manyika, Ndau, Zezuru and Korekore. Doke discovered that collectively these groups of people had no single name to describe the language they spoke and then adopted the name Shona to describe the language they speak and the people themselves. Now that we have traced the origin of the Shona people and the name Shona, its now pertinent to delve into the aspects of Shona culture, starting with how the Shona conceive a family.

1.3 The concept of the Shona family

The Shona as a people conceive of a family as *mhuri*. This *mhuri* is not quite equivalent to the European's conception of a family. We say so because in a Shona family we do not have extended family. Members often referred to as extended family members in the modern days are in actual fact family members. In the traditional Shona conception of the family, there is no nuclear nor is there an extended family. What they have is a family. Therefore, the word family in this book will be used not in the way Europeans or other Euro-centric scholars use it.

When we talk of a family in Shona, we are referring to a series of families which the Europeans might call extended families. A Shona family (*mhuri*) consists of the eldest member of that clan hence *Mhuri yekwaTatira* (Tatira family) encompasses my father, his brothers, my own brothers together with their children and wives and myself with my children and wife. The surviving eldest member of that *mhuri* is the head of that *mhuri*. If he is away the next senior to him takes over the headship.

The Shona people believe in hierarchy and that seniority goes by age not by what an individual has in terms of material possession. Senior members of the family are respected. They are normally not addressed directly but are approached through the societal hierarchy of going through the less senior and these in turn pass information until it reaches the most senior man.

At this point what is important to note is that the Shona people conceive a *mhuri* as a big cluster of relatives who come from the same clan. There is no sense, in the Shona worldview, in referring to one's father, brother, or cousin as a member of the extended family because in the Shona worldview such members are an integral part of the family unit. A Shona person would ask, 'if a grandfather becomes a member of the extended family, what then is a family? The grandfather holds influence and is the foundation of the so called nuclear family. If he is removed and relegated to the extended lot, the family becomes incomplete and ceases to function properly. In any case, in the Shona conception of a family, there is no nuclear and extended family as envisaged in the western sense. What the Shona people conceive to be a family is *mhuri* which for lack of appropriate term can be referred to as 'connected families' rather than extended. The term 'connected families' is more appropriate in reference to family. These connected families make a big family which is *mhuri*.

1.4 Responsibilities and roles of the members in the Shona family

Each member in the Shona family has responsibilities and roles one is expected to perform. The father should ensure that his family is happy and in the olden days he was supposed to provide capital to his sons for marrying their wives. The mother provides warmth both to the husband and the whole family. She is the symbol of love, warmth and care.

Boys helped in the fields as well as herding the livestock. Girls helped in the general upkeep of the homestead assisted by their mothers. Livestock namely goats and sheep were left to be looked after by younger boys of six to twelve years old while the older boys mainly looked after cattle (Tatira, 2000).

The old members of the family especially the grandfather and grandmothers were left behind in the homesteads. These functioned as repository of advice to the younger members of the family. The other role in the family was that of educating the young through *ngano* (folktales) and this function was carried out by the grandmothers. The older boys were educated through *nhango dzapadare* (advice given by grandfathers or other elderly persons outside the house at a place called *dare* (where men sit waiting for supper).

The *vana babamunini* (uncles) were also responsible for advising their brother's sons while *vana vatete* (aunts) sister to the father advised girls on how to behave well. The grandfather and grandmother had also the above as part of their responsibilities.

Boys below the age of 6, say between 3 to 5 years would remain behind in the homestead. They would be responsible for running errands assigned to them by elders who remain at home. Therefore apart from playing, the younger ones had their roles to perform at home. Children of the age of 5/6 could also be left with their youngsters whom they looked after while their parents were busy doing something.

Therefore, it can be seen that in the Shona family each member has a role to play and other members should give each member space to operate. The roles are respected and each member is expected to cooperate with the rest of the family members in order for the smooth functioning of the family. The Shona family can be compared to a corporate company where each member has a role to play for the success of the company. Each member has a role to play in the larger family hence no need to label him/her as part of the extended family but indeed is part of the family unit, with specific roles to play and responsibilities to undertake.

1.5 Changes brought about by western culture/education and religion in the Shona family

1.5.1 Western Education

In the previous discussion what we have seen was largely true among the Shona before colonialism. The western people with their western culture, religion and education brought about different thinking to the Shona people.

The curriculum taught in schools is a selection from a certain culture. What is taught in schools is the culture of a dominant group. When western education was introduced to the African, Shona people in Zimbabwe, Shona culture was deliberately and systematically left. Shona people were taught western culture at the expense of Shona culture. Most of the Shona norms and values were either not taught or discouraged at school.

Western education taught Shona people to be individualistic and selfish. The system of education also removed individuals from society and educated them out of society they normally knew. What they learnt was not known to all others whom they left at home. The social community was no longer the source of knowledge and it became irrelevant

15

to the prevailing western education system. New ideas learnt from school sometimes brought about conflict and disrespect among members of the Shona community.

The school values also conflicted with Shona societal values. At school, pupils were told to shout and stand up when greeting elders who were teachers and school administrators. Upon seeing such people entering their classrooms, they would all stand up and roar, "Good morning Sir/Madam". At home they were told to sit down and greet their elders softly. Teachers and missionaries, who were White, encouraged pupils to look straight in the elders' eyes as a sign of innocence and honesty, while at home children were not allowed to do the same. At home it was a sign of lack of good manners and respect.

The school system also implicitly taught individuals to be selfish, hence individuals were supposed to cover their work so that others would not copy. At home individuals were taught to cooperate in their tasks, hence education was facilitated through groups. Riddling was done in groups and achievements and failures were the responsibilities of all the group members not individuals. In *ngano* (folktales), the audience participated in singing and dancing, thereby contributing to the development of a plot.

Therefore, as we have seen above, western education was fundamentally different from Shona education. Members of the Shona community who were exposed to western education were bound to destabilise the Shona family. The amount of respect accorded to individuals changed, the scale which previously favoured age was tilted towards education. The more an individual was educated, the greater chances of one being respected in the family.

The educated people, though young, in some cases, assumed the role of advisors on pertinent issues which affected the family thereby unsettling the balance of power. Western education also assured the beneficiaries of good jobs therefore meant that such individuals could afford to make economic decisions without the assistance of other family members. The wife belonged to an individual rather than members of the family. The roles of *vatete, baba, mai,* and *vatete* were seemingly threatened because of economic independence of the educated Shona people. People wanted to live as individuals, determining their destiny. This resulted in daughter–in-laws and sons-in-laws not giving enough respect to their respective in-laws, hence the acceptance of the term extended family. Advice which was previously sought after by the young people married is, in some cases, no longer welcome. The advice from elders is more often than not branded interferences. The roles the father, mother, brother, nephew, cousin, grandfather/mother and other relatives they traditionally used to play are either marginalized or avoided.

Kahari (1972:11) writing on how western education impacted on Chakaipa, he notes,

> His studies naturally led him into another world– a world
>
> of western thought, philosophy and industrialisation. His native
>
> imagination immediately came to grips with environment, which
>
> appreciated individual liberty and development as opposed to group
>
> development.

Finally let us see how western religion impacted negatively in the Shona family. This phenomenon is fully articulated in the next subsection.

1.5.2 Western Religion

The western religion came and abolished some of the practices of the Shona people. Some of the things which assisted the Shona family to remain intact were challenged and dismissed as pagan practices. The appeasement of the ancestral spirits apart from its religious functions, which are in no doubt contested and controversial helped the Shona family to keep in touch as family members met from time to time to appease their ancestral spirits. The family members worked together for the common good of their ancestral spirits. The regular brewing of beer for the ancestral spirits helped members of the connected families to remain in touch and to share problems and successes together. The occasion provided for a family public forum to deliberate as a larger group on problems that were believed to affect the family. In some cases the forum functioned as a counselling session for some family members.

Such gathering constantly reminded family members of the need to respect the elder members of the family. This is so because the responsibility and legitimacy to communicate with the ancestral spirits was vested on the elder member who did this on behalf of the whole family. Such vested function ensured that members within the family rally behind their seniors thereby sustaining the status quo.

However with the advent of Christianity, the Shona family was threatened. True Christians no longer believe in the appeasement of ancestral spirits. The respect of the senior member's position with regards to the spiritual world has been usurped by the church minister. Whenever a Christian is threatened, say he/she needs counselling, the church is likely to be the first port of call. Other confused Christians even go to the extent of rejecting their parents on the ground that they are heathen. In such cases, the influence of senior members of the family who are perceived not to be Christians is non-existent.

The other important belief which helped the family to leave in harmony was the belief in *Kutanda botso* (a belief that a wronged mother when she dies, her spirit comes back to torment the child who wronged her). In traditional Shona religion, you atone for your sins while you are here on earth. If one ill-treats his/her mother, the perpetrator is tormented by the spirit (Tatira, 2000b). This belief helped the Shona members to remain respectful and caring for the mothers. Christians do not believe in *ngozi* (avenging spirits) and the ancestral spirits. This means that, theoretically, even the mother can be ill-treated without any fear of *ngozi* (avenging spirit) among the Christians, though obviously Christians are bound by their Christian ethos not to ill-treat parents. Above all the whole mark of Christian teaching is love.

1.6 Summary

This chapter has taken the discussion through the important stages which are as follows;

- That the Shona are part of the people called the Bantu.
- Shona people like other Bantu tribes migrated from the north of Africa to the south of Africa.
- The group that is now known as the Shona people briefly settled in Tanzania (Guruuswa) before proceeding to the present day Zimbabwe.
- One view postulates that in Tanzania the group split into two, the first to leave Tanzania being the Dziva-Hungwe and the Mbire (Shona) followed later.
- Another view was that the Mbire and Dziva–Hungwe were never an integral group, they migrated separately.

- The first view is advanced by Mutswairo (1996) while the second view is advanced by Chigwedere (1980).

- The name Shona was not an indigenous name for the indigenous people of Zimbabwe. This was a label for the Rozvi people by outsiders, originally used by the Ndebele and adopted by the Europeans. It is Doke who gave it legitimacy when he crafted his 1930 Shona Orthography.

- The conception of a family among the Shona is different from that of Europeans.

- Every member of the Shona family has roles and responsibilities accorded to him/her thus according him/her functions in a larger family (*mhuri*).

- The school has impacted negatively on the Shona family by its different ideology which, in some cases, subverts the Shona values and norms.

- Western religion has impacted negatively by destroying the Shona belief system which fostered on cohesion of the family in favour of divisive, individualistic approach to religion and life in general.

Chapter 2

2.0 The Marriage

2.1 Introduction

The institution of marriage is as old as the Shona people themselves. Marriage among the Shona people, is an important phenomenon and almost a compulsory exercise to members of the Shona society. Once one remains single past the expected marriageable age, one is bothered by relatives, and even non-relatives why one is not marrying. There is a social stigma attached to people who remain single beyond the expected age of marrying. Marrying is a social obligation among the Shona people.

Marriage is seen as important because it ensures the continuation of families and clans. Families are custodians of culture and safety nets to fall on in times of trials. Families provide social security to the old and the sick. Shona people view a family as an investment in the economic sense, hence the Shona proverb, *Chirere mangwana chigokurerawo* (Look after him/her so that in future he/she will do the same).

In Shona society, one is never an adult until one gets married. Through marriage, members of the Shona society graduate from one phase of being single, which is marked by less responsibility to another phase that is characterised by more social responsibility. Through marriage, one gains respect and dignity in the community. The social status of being married automatically qualifies an individual to be addressed in the honorific plural *Va-* for Mr when referring to male members and *Mai* for Mrs when referring to females members.

Because of the importance and the central function marriage plays in the survival of the Shona society, important procedures should be undertaken and followed before one is said to be married. Let us now investigate what constitute marriage among the Shona.

2.2 What is marriage?

Among the Shona marriage is said to have taken place when two families come together and sanctify the union of two lovers. The sanctification comes about when the male family pays lobola to the female family. On the same phenomenon, Masasire in Mutswairo et al (1996:42) explains,

> ... marriage is brought about only by the transfer of *roora*/bride wealth,
> in the form of cattle and money nowadays, from agnatic group of the groom
> to that of the bride.

As can be seen from the above, marriage is not a contract between the two individuals but between two different families. The same is observed by Redcliffe-Brown and Forde (1950:51) they note, "In Africa a marriage is not simply a union of a man and a woman. It is an alliance between the two families or bodies of kin". It is only after negotiations and payments are made to the satisfaction of the in-laws that the wife is given to his husband. When this happens, we say marriage has taken place. It is possible that an individual can stay with a woman and even fathers the women but without having paid lobola, though they can live together for many years, these people are not married.

The Shona people traditionally prove the point further that a wife is not married to an individual by handing over the wife to the father of the groom or brother only after the payments are made. The father/brother to whom the wife is handed to, represent the family. Any disputes which threaten marriage are presided over by these senior members of the family. In the case of divorce, almost the same group of people who presided over the marriage is the one which dissolves the marriage.

Therefore, traditionally, among the Shona, neither marriage nor divorce is a private affair to be executed by two lone lovers but is an issue which attracts involvement of many family members from both sides. This process ensured stability of marriage. One had to think twice and consult widely before one could think of divorce. This is one of the reasons why previously marriage lasted than what is happening these days.

2.3 Traditional ways of getting married

There are many traditional ways of getting married among the Shona, some of them are still practiced while others have since either fallen out of pace with time or abolished by the law. In this section we shall look at all these ways of getting married even though some are not practiced these days. The following are the traditional ways of getting married:

a) Marriage by means of working for a father-in-law in return for a wife (*Kutema ugariri*).

b) Marriage by self imposition *(Kuganha)*.

c) Marriage by forcibly lifting a woman to one's home *(Musengabere)*.

d) Marriage through child pledging *(Kuzvarira)*.

e) Marriage by throwing a log at the prospective in-law's homestead *(Kukanda mutanda)*.

f) Marriage by replacing a dead aunt/sister *(Chimutsamapfihwa)*.

g) Marriage by elopement *(Kutizira/Kutizisa)*.

h) Marriage by negotiation *(Kukumbira)*.

Among all the ways given above, the most popular and most practiced are marriage through negotiation *(Kukumbira)* and marriage by elopement *(Kutizira/Kutizisa)* (Gombe,1986).

At this juncture we would like to discuss in detail the different ways of getting married. We start with marriage by means of working for the father-in-law in return for a wife hereafter called *Kutema ugariri*.

2.3.1 *Kutema ugariri* (Marriage by means of working for the father-in-law in return for a wife)

This is an old practice which was not only confined to the Africans. Even in the Bible, the Jews used to marry through this practice. This is how Jacob got his wives from Laban.

In traditional society, this practice was mostly embraced by the poor man in society who had no capital to marry. Usually such people were orphans. Traditionally as you might know, the father was responsible for paying lobola for the son's wife, therefore in the event of the father's death the orphan might have been left without a start and had to work for a wife.

The practice enabled the poor to marry as long as one was hard-working and honest. The poor were considered like any other human beings with dreams and ambitions to fulfill, hence a Shona proverb, *Murombo munhu* (A poor person is still a human being).

This means the poor has desires as any other person and should be afforded the chance to progress in life like any other person. The person who was poor was supposed to send a *munyai* (an intermediary) to go and approach his in-laws telling them of his intention to marry. The man was expected to give a small token to the *munyai* (intermediary) to enable him to initiate the dialogue with his in-laws.

After a successful dialogue, the man was supposed to join his in-law's family and work for him for a stipulated period. The work given to the son-in-law was trying. One could be asked to clear a thicket and prepare it for planting. The in-law was supposed to prove his salt by producing a bumper harvest. In some cases the son-in-law was supposed to work for five to seven years before one was given a wife. The time was shortened if the son-in-law was very hard-working and respectful, never complained but worked extra miles to have tasks performed in time and to perfection. *Kutema ugariri* was sort of a test to prove how committed and prepared the son-in-law was to work for his wife. Some lazy people ran away from their father-in-laws without a wife when the going got tough.

During the period of working under the father-in-law, the son-in-law was not expected to be husband to his wife until he was given the wife. After completing serving his father-in-law, the man was given his wife. However, the man was supposed to give her mother-in-law *mombe yeumai* (beast). This meant that he could work for a certain period to be given that beast which he was to give to the mother-in-law. If the beast could not be found, a goat or two could do as substitutes.

2.3.2 *Kuganha* (Marriage by self imposition)

This way of getting married, seems strange these days but it used to be practiced in the past. This was only used by women to men and not vice-versa. A woman who had deep love for a bachelor or even a married man would go straight to the home of the person she loved. The woman would go to the person she loved, not because the man had proposed love to her but simply because she had an urge to be married by that particular individual. Most often, such a man chosen by the woman was an upright man in the society that he became the subject of talk in the society.

23

Before the woman imposed herself to the man, she would have done everything possible to lure the man to initiate love dialogue without success. It is only after numerous unsuccessful attempts that the woman decided to go and impose herself to the man. The woman would tell her intention to her aunt or sometimes the mother before she goes to the man so that they will not look for her.

The woman would then sit at the border of the man's yard with all her belongings. People would ask her the purpose of the visit which she would explain. The family members would be summoned to a gathering to discuss the issue. Usually such a gathering was done a day after the woman's arrival. It was possible that the man would refuse to marry the woman but elders would normally persuade him not to reject the woman. Elders would argue that the woman was sent by the ancestral spirits. To reject her would be to reject the offer of the ancestral spirits and this would anger such spirits.

If the man was a bachelor, he was allowed to marry other women of his own choice apart from this one from *vadzimu* (ancestral spirits). The grounds for refusal were therefore limited as it were. If the man remained adamant, and refused to marry the woman, he was taken to a chief's court where he was supposed to pay a fine in cattle. We should emphasise that such rejections rarely happened because women unlike these days were married for their good behaviour and for the reason that they would produce children. There were no materialistic strings to consider in marriage, like the level of education and the woman's profession as what happens these days. Beauty was also insignificant because physical beauty was held with mistrust hence the following proverbs, *Mukadzi munaku akasaroya anoba* (A beautiful woman if she is not a witch she is a thief) and *Matende mashava mavazva doro* (Beautiful woman spoil peace).

Finally it was also a prestigious thing to have a woman only coming specifically to you in the whole village full of other people. The occasion was mostly readily accepted with an amount of celebration and humility.

2.3.3 *Musengabere* (Marriage by forcibly lifting a woman to one's home)

This involves the physical lifting of a woman one desires to marry to his home. What would happen is that a man in company of his friends, would connive to bundle and carry a woman he loved to his place. These people would carry out their exercise at a lonely place, possibly at a well or in a forest when the woman is alone or with her sister.

The woman would beat, bite, kick these men to free herself from them but the men needed to be strong to withstand all these. This exercise was not done by strangers to a stranger. The man would be known to the woman. In most cases, the man would have proposed love before but the woman would have dilly dallied. Soon the gentleman would discover that the woman loves her but was not coming in the open. The only option left was to lift her to his home and to finish the courtship with the assistance of his relatives.

On arrival, the woman was locked in the man's room. Aunts and sisters to the man would stay with the woman, meanwhile persuading her to love the man. Two to four days could pass while persuasion went on. After some time the woman normally accepted and normal procedures of marrying were taken.

One view which can also be correct is that in some cases, this type of marriage was resorted to by men who failed to attract relationships with women. After having failed to get a woman when one came of age, one would resort to *Musengabere* (Marriage by forcibly lifting a woman to one's home). In this case, the man did not necessarily need to pick a woman he once proposed. What was important was that the two were not complete strangers to each other. If people just picked at random, it was possible to pick someone's wife or an 'engaged' woman. The system would have created problems which were complicated to solve.

2.3.4 *Kuzvarira* (Child pledging)

This was normally necessitated by a crisis in a family. Common crisis was that of hunger. A girl child was normally given at birth, before birth or after birth to a rich man in society in return for food. Sometimes the father of the girl would have committed a crime which required him to pay a fine in the form of cattle. He would approach a rich man to give him cattle in exchange of his daughter.

From the time the deal was sealed, the child was someone else's wife. If the child decided to marry another man, the father was to pay a heavy fine to the rich man. In the olden days, the wronged husband could go to the extent of enlisting the help of a diviner. This diviner would hurt the husband who took the wife by lightning (*kurovesa nemheni*) or by having the husband stung to death by bees (*kurumisa nenyuchi*). Therefore, it was difficult for the pledged daughter to get a husband apart from the one pledged by the father. The Shona people have a strong belief that, *tsvingu ine ngozi* (Marriying someone's wife puts you into troubles).

2.3.5 *Kukanda mutanda* (Marriage by throwing a log at the prospective in-law's homestead)

This type of marriage can be equated to the present lay bye we find in shops. It was a sort of a security deposit, a claim to ownership. What used to happen was that when a man knew that in a village, there was a baby girl, an interested man would go with a log.

Upon arrival, the man would drop the log close to the kitchen in a way that it made noise as it dropped. The mother of the newly born baby would check to see the person who brought the log. If she was happy, she accepted the man as her in-law. The acceptance of the in-law was expressed by using the deposited log. If she did not accept the in-law, the log would remain unused and the owner would know that his request to marry was turned down. The owner of the used log would proceed with the payment of lobola in due course, but from the time the log was used, the girl was known as someone else's wife.

2.3.6 *Chimutsamapfihwa* (Marriage by replacing a dead aunt/sister)

This form of marriage is still practiced by others even today. In the event of a wife's death, the in-laws can give their son-in-law another wife to look after the children left by the deceased. In order for the son-in-law to be given another wife, he should have paid lobola for his deceased wife to the satisfaction of his in-laws.

The wife who is given to the son-in-law might be the deceased's younger sister or daughter of the deceased's brother. In marrying such a wife, very little lobola was paid to the in-laws if the son-in-law had finished lobola for the late wife.

Though this practice is still practiced by others, it is no longer popular because of the fear of AIDS. Parents are no longer willing to risk their children by marrying them to people who have lost their spouses. The practice also fell out of favour before the AIDS pandemic took root in Zimbabwe because of the changes brought about by western education and Christianity.

Educated young women often prefer to choose their own husbands as opposed to be given to widowers. Some husbands also like to look for their own spouses after the death of their wives. More reasons as to why marriage by replacing a dead aunt/sister is not so popular these days will be discussed when we look at the impact of foreign influence on marriages.

2.3.7 *Kutiza mukumbo/Kutiziswa mukumbo* (elopement)

This way of marrying is still prevalent among the Shona people. Some prefer it as they say is a quicker and easier way of marrying. However others do not like it citing that things should be done openly not through the cover of darkness. Anywhere, there are two types of elopement. One that is initiated by the girl alone without the lover's knowledge or approval, while the other one is a neatly arranged procedure which is done with the full knowledge and approval of the lover and some selected relatives from both sides. These selected relatives facilitate the exercise.

The woman elopes secretly to her lover, normally when she falls pregnant. She does so because the man who would be responsible for the pregnancy would be delaying or refusing to facilitate the marriage arrangements. In the Shona culture, it is taboo for a woman to remain at her father's place while pregnant without having been married. The situation demands that the woman goes to the man responsible.

The woman would pack all her belongings and go alone or most likely with her aunt to the man responsible. The woman would sit on the border of the yard while covering her head with a piece of cloth. She would tell the elders who attend to her that she is their permanent visitor. Since this normally happens close to sunset, people would normally go to sleep without discussing anything serious.

On the following morning, members of the family would be summoned to deliberate on the issue. The implicated man would be asked about the claims of the woman.

27

Sometimes the man would accept responsibility without any argument. However, it is not unusual for a man to deny responsibility, but senior members of the family would usually put pressure on him to accept responsibility. They would assess his statements against the woman's submissions and, in most cases, dismiss them as baseless. We should take note of the fact that in the olden days, it was rare for women to make false claims on men regarding paternity.

The second type of elopement is that which is done through mutual consent, where the woman confides with her aunt and sisters of her intention. The mother can also be told though she would pretend to know nothing even if the husband asks her the whereabouts of their daughter. Meanwhile, on the other side, the man also confides with his sisters and aunts about his intention of bringing his lady home through *kutizira* (elopement)

The exercise takes place during *chirimo* (the dry season) at night when there is *jenaguru* (a full blown moon). The point of taking off is usually near the cattle kraal. This place is convenient because it is not too far neither is it too close to the homestead. People can converse without being heard by others who will be sleeping at home. They can too easily go back to bed if the other part fails to fulfill the promise.

Long back, the male relatives would bring food, usually rapoko, sadza and chicken. Both parties would eat and then after eating embark on their journey. The woman would make frequent stops and would be given money by relatives of her lover so that she continues with the journey. She might refuse to cross a path, a river or stream unless given something. This would continue until she reaches the home of her lover. Some money would be paid to let her enter into the yard, then hut and then to open the veil which will be covering her face. Such money will be used to buy utensils for her use.

After a week or some days, a *munyai* (intermediary) would be send to inform the in-laws of the intention to pay lobola. The *munyai* (intermediary) would pretend to be just visiting and chats with the father-in-law. After a while, he would hide a token and leaves the premises. He would then shout *(kudanidzira)*, from a safe distance that he left a token for them. He would tell them where to look for their daughter.

Long back one would have to be an accomplished athlete because, the father or brothers of the girl would run after the *munyai* (intermediary). If caught, he would be severely beaten. The other would be for the *munyai* (intermediary) to visit the girl's father early in the morning while he was still in bed. He would shout *(kudanidzira)* the purpose of his visit, quickly leaves the token at the door step, and runs away. However, things have changed these days, it is now common for the *munyai* (intermediary) to talk to the *tezvara* (in-law) directly informing him where his daughter is and the intentions of the in-laws to marry. After some months, the process of paying lobolo is then negotiated.

2.3.8 *Kukumbira* (Marriage by negotiation)

Of all the ways of getting married, this found the approval of the missionaries when they Christianised the Shona. To date, this way of getting married is the one which is encouraged by the Christian churches.

When an individual wants to marry through *kukumbira* (negotiation), he informs his uncle, brother to his father, of his plans. A token fee is paid which will be handed to inform the man's father that his son intends to marry. The woman who is to be married also informs her aunt of her intention to get married and look for a *munyai* (intermediary) they will recommend to the man's family. This *munyai* (intermediary) will take the man's family to the woman's family to initiate the dialogue. The *munyai* (intermediary) should be a friend to the woman's father.

On an agreed date, a small delegation is send to the woman's home to negotiate marriage. The delegation goes to the *munyai* (intermediary), who will take them to their in-laws. Negotiations can start with the man's delegation being left in the bush or anywhere close to the in-law's homestead. The *munyai* (intermediary) moves back and forth until the delegation is allowed entry into the homestead, for a fee of course.

Negotiations continue in the homestead but in separate dwelling with the *munyai* (intermediary) moving back and forth. It is only after the deal has been sealed that the man's delegation is invited to come in the kitchen or any other place where the in-laws would be. They would be invited to greet the in-laws (*kuchuchira vana baba naanaambuya*). A small token is placed in the plate or whatever container is used to inform the in-laws that the man's delegation wants to greet them.

2.4 Bride wealth

At this point let us see into detail things which a man who is getting married is asked to pay by his in-laws. There is a general guideline which can differ from area to area and from family to family. These payments are paid when one either marry through *kukumbira* (negotiation) or *kutizisa* (elopement). The only difference will be on the amounts of money charged per each stage. *Kukumbira* attracts heft payments while *kutizisa* attracts lower payments.

First before the son-in-law pays anything, he is asked to pay *zvibinge* (small fines charged as part of marriage proceedings by the in-laws to a son-in-law). Below are some names of the *zvibinge* (small fines charged as part of marriage proceedings by the in-laws to a son-in-law) that are charged:

a) *Vhuramuromo* (Money paid to initiate dialogue).

b) *Wakandinzwanani* (Money paid by a son-in-law as a fine to the father-in-law for having known that the father- in- law has a daughter).

c) *Matekenyandebvu* (Money paid by a son-in-law as a fine to a father-in-law because the woman to be married used to pull her father's beard when she was young).

d) *Mari yerambi* (Money paid as a fine to a mother-in-law by a son-in-law for having used her candles during the night when she used to attend to the woman to be married when she cried at night as a baby).

e) *Kapadza* (Money paid as a fine by a son-in-law to a mother-in law for a small hole she used to dig roots to treat the woman to be married when she was a baby).

f) *Mbereko* (Money paid by a son-in-law to a mother-in-law for having bought a back-sling to carry the woman to be married when she was a baby).

g) *Mhwanyaruzhowa* (Money charged as fine to a son-in-law, on the assumption that the son-in-law would have had unsanctified visits to the father-in-law's homestead during courtship and many times using unsanctioned entry and exit points to avoid being seen).

h) *Mavhuna* (Money paid as a fine by a son-in-law if the woman is already pregnant when he pays lobola).

30

i) *Mari yedare* (Money paid by a son-in-law meant for the male members of the in-laws who constitute a panel that deliberate on the proceedings when one pays lobolo).

j) *Kusunga mukarabwa* (Money paid by a son-in-law meant for one of the brothers to the woman to be married). This brother-in-law is supposed to be the reference point, he stands for the father-in-law.

There is no limit to these fines, the in-law can even say, for example, "You once saw me and did not greet me". A son-in-law is then ordered to pay a fine. The assumption is that during courtship, the chances are that the son-in-law might have met the father-in law, and avoided greeting him because it was improper for him to do so. We will discuss the rationale for all the fines in Shona culture.

After the *zvibinge* (small fines charged as part of marriage proceedings by the in-laws to a son-in-law), the in-laws are asked to put money in *tswanda* (a winnowing tray) for a selected group of woman's relatives to pick *(kunonga)*. Those who normally pick are sisters and aunts. The woman who is to be married also picks. Normally, she is the one who picks the largest amount, followed by the aunt and sisters. The money picked should be used to buy utensils which will help the woman to start her new home.

In the just discussed exercise, we find that most of the proceeds go to the womenfolk. The father-in-law gets the actual *roora* (bride wealth). All the just discussed payments are not *roora* (bride wealth). If a son-in-law fails to go beyond this stage, he is said not to have married and the father-in-law is not at liberty to give him his daughter. It is normal to return to the son-in-law everything he has paid and ask him to come back after he has properly prepared himself. However, such incidents are rare since the son-in-law would have carried out some research about the likely charges. When he goes to pay lobolo, he would have prepared himself that he goes with cash which takes him beyond the elementary stages of *zvibinge* (small fines charged as part of the marriage proceedings by the in-laws to a son-in-law).

The father-in-law charges *rugaba/rusambo* (bride wealth). This is money for the father-in-law which, traditionally, he could use as per his discretion. The father-in-law also charges his son-in-law *danga* (cattle) or money instead of live cattle but the money still represents *danga* (cattle). However, in most cases, the mother-in-law's *mombe yeumai* (a heir paid to the mother-in-law) is not substituted by money. The in-law can be asked to bring it alive or to leave cash with the in-laws of equivalent value to a live beast. The money is then used to purchase a live beast for the mother-in-law.

There is a strong belief that the mother-in-law's beast is given to her in custody of her ancestral spirits which are believed to be responsible for the fertility of the wife. There is also *imbwazukuru* (a goat paid by a son-in-law given to a maternal grandmother). Both mombe yeumai and imbwazukuru are given the maternal side of the married woman. The reason being that the maternal spirits control the fertility of the married woman and if such things are not provided for, such spirits will cause infertility to the woman or any other misfortunes related to childbirth.

Lastly there are *majasi* (clothes for the father-in-law and mother-in-law). The father-in – law normally gives to the son-in-law a list which generally includes the following:

a) For himself; hat, suit, belt, shirt, one pair of shoes, stockings, tie and an overcoat

b) For his wife; dress, in other cases a costume and a blouse, head-cover, overcoat, a pair of shoes, stockings, jug and *chari* (a piece of cloth/small blanket for wrapping oneself, especially from the waist to the legs.

It should be emphasised that all the transactions are presided over by the *munyai* (intermediary), not that the in-laws talk directly to each other. All the listed things cannot normally be paid in a single day or years but over a number of years. However, in order for one to be given his wife and for him to be considered married, he should have paid part of *rugaba* (bride wealth) and *danga* (cattle). For those who want to wed, they should have finished buying the clothes for the father-in-law and the mother-in-law. If such clothes are not supplied, the in-laws will say that they cannot attend the wedding while naked. They argue that they need to be clothed first before the wedding takes place.

At this juncture, it is pertinent to clear some of the questions which might have been puzzling the minds of young and/or westernised readers on the rationality of all the *zvibinge* (small fines charged as part of marriage proceedings by the in-laws to a son-in-law).

2.5 Why Zvibinge? (Small fines charged as part of marriage proceedings by the in-laws to the son-in-law)

Zvibinge (Small fines charged as part of marriage proceedings by the in-laws to the son-in-law) are tests, more like those trying assignments given to a son-in-law who works for a wife under his father-in -law. They are paid to prove that one loves his wife. One is asked to assume responsibility for his wife from the start. This is an initiation to the long life of responsibility in marriage. The husband is asked to pay fines for acts he did not commit and some which are said to have been committed by his wife when she was a baby. Some of the things seem nonsensical but nevertheless fines are supposed to be paid.

It is not uncommon in Shona society for a man to be accountable for acts of his wife and children. The Shona people know very well that a married woman is protected by her husband thus the sayings, *Mukadzi wemunhu haagadzwi dare murume wake asipo* (You cannot preside over a case involving a married woman in the absence of her husband) and *Isimba kaviri kurwa nemukadzi weasipo* (You have to fight twice if you fight a married woman).

The idea of *zvibinge* (small fines charged as part of marriage proceedings by the in-laws to a son-in-law), transfer the responsibility of looking after the woman from the father to a husband. Traditionally, when a woman is single the father is held accountable for the misdeeds of her daughter, now that she is married the husband takes over the responsibility. The idea of fining the son-in-law also brings the son-in-law into the realisation that a father-in-law should be respected and if he goes over bounds in future he will be liable to other fines. This helps the son-in-law to know his bounds.

Finally such fines help to educate the son-in-law to be humble and conforming. He is taught through such fines that in life, one sometimes has to do things though he might not be interested in doing so. Sometimes things have to be done for the common good of others without philosophising on issues. In life, specifically in Shona upbringing, it does not mean that everything they do must be things they like or agree with. In some instances, they have to do things they do not like or agree with because a senior person wants it done. As long as that thing is not bad, that thing should be done as a sign of respect and in order to maintain harmony among people. Harmony is a golden rule among the Shona people. Above all, one is taught where and when to argue and where and when not to argue.

2.6 The impact of foreign influence on the ways of getting married among the Shona

The ways of getting married through *kuzvarira* (child pledging), *kuganha* (marriage by self imposition), *kukanda mutanda* (marrying by throwing a log at the prospective in-law's homestead), *musengabere* (marriage by forcibly lifting a woman to one's home), *chimutsamapfiwa* (marriage by replacing a dead wife by a sister/aunt) and *kutema ugariri* (marrying by working for a father-in law in return for a wife), have all since ceased being practiced except *chimutsamapfiwa* (marriage by replacing a dead wife by a sister/aunt) which is practiced to a less extend.

As people mix with other people from different cultures, some of their cultural practices are bound to change or cease to function. The colonial government also made direct intervention on some of the practices. The system of *kuzvarira* (child pledging) as a way of marriage, was abolished as far back as 1898 by the African Marriage Act.

This Act as cited in Weinrich (1982:62) reads;

> Any contract or agreement made under which any girl is in
> consideration of any payment, loan or gift promised in marriage to
> any man shall not be enforced in law unless the girl is of marriageable
> age and consents to the union.

The above cited Act also nullified the practice of *kukanda mutanda* (marriage by throwing a log at the prospective in-law's homestead). The existence of the Act did not mean that the Shona people stopped child pledging, the practice is said to have continued for some time but through education, girls resisted the practice.

There are also laws which protect people from *musengabere* (marriage by forcibly lifting a woman to one's home). Such people will be charged with abduction or kidnapping, sexual abuse or unlawful detention among other charges. Such ways of getting married have failed to withstand the test of time. Through the influence of western education,

34

sensibilities have changed. What used to be accepted has been challenged as violating human rights and woman dignity.

Therefore, it can be concluded that most forms of marriage apart from *kutizira/kutiziswa* (elopement) and *kukumbira* (negotiation) have either died a natural death or have been forced out of use by systematic legislation.

2.7 Summary

The chapter interrogated a lot of issues pertaining to Shona marriages and some of the main issues which stand out are as follows:

- Among the Shona people and indeed African people, marriage is a bond which ties two families together and is viewed as a co-operate exercise rather than an individual undertaking.

- One is considered married, only after one has paid *roora* (bride wealth) to his in-laws.

- Marriage, since it is a co-operate exercise in Shona culture, when one divorces, the dissolution of marriage is normally done by a selected group of relatives from both sides of the in-laws.

- Traditionally, there were many ways of getting married but most of them have ceased to function.

- The most employed ways are of getting married are *kutizira/ kutiziswa mukumbo* (elopement) and *kukumbira* (marriage by negotiation).

- *Roora* (Bride wealth) is an important aspect in marriage, for it legitimises the union of the two.

- *Zvibinge* (small fines charged as part of the marriage proceeding by the in-laws to the son-in-law) have important functions in the process of marriage, for they intend to regulate the son-in-law's behaviour and also indirectly initiate him into marriage responsibilities.

Chapter 3

3.0 The Shona Traditional Religion

3.1 Introduction

The Shona people like any other people have the quest for belonging. The quest gives rise to religious beliefs. The Shona as a people, have a religion which seeks to explain the supernatural power which controls or influences their environment. They seek to control or influence these powers with rituals and ceremonies.

The Shona people perform rituals when faced with catastrophe. When there is drought or numerous deaths, the Shona people perform rituals to appease the spirits so that there is an end to such mishaps. The uncertainty of life or the unknown are explained through beliefs. Life after death is explained through the beliefs of *midzimu* (ancestral spirits). Illness can be explained by the beliefs in *uroyi* (witchcraft) or *ngozi* (avenging spirits) depending on the type of such illness.

With Shona religious beliefs, man can explain his destiny and other things that might threaten his existence on earth. Through such beliefs, man masters powers which control his environment and therefore man becomes psychologically balanced and can better face the present and future.

Far from the Conradian belief that Africans, Shona included, have no religion and lack the concept of *Mwari* (God), the Shona people have a strong concept of *Mwari* (God). The Shona people believe that on the highest rung of their beliefs, there is a creator of all things who is *Mwari* (God). The Shona have various names for this *Mwari* (God). Therefore, without wasting time, let us see the Shona people's concept of God.

3.2 The Shona Concept of *Mwari* (God)

The Shona people believe in *Mwari* (God) as the creator and originator of all things. They believe in one *Mwari* (God) and as a result they are monotheist, contrary to the western view which regarded them as animistic. In support of the view that the Shona people are monotheist, Zvarevashe in Clive and Peggy Kileff (1970:44) observes,

Shona–speaking people are monotheist and their religion is complex. It is complicated by the fact that although they believe in God (*Mwari*) they also believe that their lives are controlled by the ancestral spirits (*vadzimu*).

The complexity of Shona religion made western scholars to come up with erroneous conclusion of the Shona beliefs. Some western scholars thought that the Shona worship animals, plants and other objects and that the Shona had no concept of God. This is far from the truth as we shall see.

Contrary to all these views, the Shona people view *Mwari* (God) as someone who is up there and one who is very senior, as a result he should not bothered with less important issues. The Shona believe that they can communicate with God through their ancestral spirits. According to their belief, it is improper to by-pass the ancestral spirits, and communicate directly with God. In fact, the Shona believe that such an address will be ignored by God.

Even in the Shona people's day-to-day affairs, handling of issues is done through a certain hierarchy. Issues are communicated through the junior person until they reach the most senior person. Take for example when one arrives at a village gathering, one has to pass his greetings to the seniors through the junior members of the gathering. A junior member, for example, would say, *Eh Madyirapazhe, mwana anoda kukumhorosai* (Eh Madyirapazhe, someone wants to greet you). One is not supposed to directly greet seniors in society especially chiefs, village heads or headmen, one greets them through their aides or their juniors.

The same can happen in a family, for instance there are certain issues which go through the mother then the father. Other issues go straight to the father through certain relatives. In the case of a young man informing the father that he intends to marry, he approaches his uncle, a younger brother to his father, as we have discussed in the previous chapter when touched on marriage.

Some readers might be baffled and be quick to say that this is a primitive way of communicating. They might be puzzled as to why the Shona do not communicate directly. I should emphasise that even modern societies operate in the same way in some instances. The modern society calls this type of communication bureaucracy. It is not uncommon to find that teachers are not allowed to communicate directly with their district, regional and head offices. Therefore communication is from the lowest rung up to the highest rung and not direct from the lowest to the highest rung.

Therefore, in the Shona belief system, God exists but He should not be communicated directly with the people. A diagram below shows the position of God.

GOD (*MWARI*)

Tribal spirits

Family spirits

Living people

Apart from knowing that God occupies the highest rung in the Shona spiritual beliefs, the Shona people have different names for God which express how they conceive Him.

Shona people call God *Musiki* (The Creator). God is the creator of all things as revealed by the name *Musiki*. Related to this Mbiti in Masoko (1994:105) explains,

> Expressed ontologically, God is the origin and sustenance of all
> things. He is older than Zamani (Swahili word for "past") period,
> He is outside and beyond his creation. On the other hand, He is
> personally involved in His creation, so that it is not outside Him

or His reach. God is thus simultaneously transcendent and immenant…

Nyadenga (Owner of the sky/one who resides up there). The Shona believe that God is the owner of the sky or skies (*Samatenga*). He is up there and controls the earth from above. He is the provider of rain since He is the owner of the skies.

According to the Shona beliefs, God is all powerful hence the name *Samasimba* (The all powerful). He controls everything. He is also the provider and can withhold blessings hence the name *Chirozvamauya* (One who withholds blessings). At the same time God is someone who is dreaded hence the name *Chikara* (The dreaded one). God's depth cannot be measured hence the name *Dzivaguru* (Deep pool). Some of the names are not in frequent use, but names like *Nyadenga* (Owner of the sky), *Musiki* (Creator), and *Samasimba* (The all powerful) are in common use. The names for God for the Shona people show certain characteristics which the Shona attribute to God. Through the names it is evident that the Shona believe that God is the creator, provider of rain, and is all powerful hence controls the fate of people.

3.3 Family spirits (*Va[Mi]dzimu*)

Like every individual who has a shadow that follows him/her everywhere, so the Shona believe that every individual family has an ancestral spirit which protects its family members wherever they are. Gelfand (1977) notes that most important of *vadzimu* (ancestral spirits) is the spirit (*mudzimu*) of the dead paternal grandfather (*sekuru*). The *sekuru* (grandfather), is believed to be responsible for the protection of all its grandchildren from illness, especially from *uroyi* (witchcraft) and any other misfortunes. As the father in his physical existence is supposed to protect his family from adversaries so is the grandfather in his spiritual existence.

The family members should be careful not to annoy the ancestral spirits lest they let enemies free to torment the agnates. The family members should therefore keep *vadzimu* (ancestral spirits) happy by frequently brewing beer in honour of these *vadzimu* (ancestral spirits). All important decisions or developments in the family must be made known to the *vadzimu* (ancestral spirits). It is not an uncommon practice to keep a bull (*gono remusha*) which is consecrated to the deceased grandfather and is named after him. The bull (*gono remusha*) is normally kept by the eldest brother in the family, who communicates with the spirit on behalf of the whole family. The ancestral spirit is believed to reside in the bull. It should be noted that it is not the physical bull which the Shona believe they will be addressing, but they believe that they are addressing the ancestral spirit which they believe entered the bull the time it was consecrated to the deceased person. Missionaries failed to understand this and they thought Shona people were animalistic.

An address to the ancestral spirits is usually done early in the morning just before sunrise. It is generally the eldest brother in the family, who will go to the kraal with rapoko grain or snuff to address the bull as though one is addressing a real person. He says what he wants to the ancestral spirit. At the end of his address, the family members clasp hands and women ululate. It is not always that people go to the kraal, sometimes the address to the ancestors is done in a round hut.

Below are some of the occasions a Shona family might communicate with their ancestors,

a) Before a family member sets off for a long journey, for example, leaving rural areas for the city, leaving Zimbabwe for a foreign country or a child leaving home for a boarding school.

b) When a child is sick.

c) When setting off to consult a n'anga.

d) When a daughter is leaving home to join her husband's family.

e) When a beast is bought, thus added to the existing herd.

f) When a beast is sold, thus subtracted from the existing herd.

g) When a baby is born.

h) When going to pay lobolo for a wife.

i) When a just married woman arrives to her husband's home.

All the above communications are made by the most senior member of the family who might be a father or an eldest brother. It is a common belief that the ancestral spirits can make their demands known to their agnates by making a family member ill. The relatives of the ill person are expected to subsequently consult a *n'anga* (diviner), who would diagnose the illness and tell the relatives that they should brew beer for the ancestors.

The illness could have occurred because the agnates have not informed the spirits of certain important issues in the family as listed before. Sometimes it could be that the ancestors simply want to be remembered through the brewing of beer. After the brewing of the beer the ill person may recover. It is believed that if people refuse to take heed to the ancestral spirits' demands, the person can die or go insane. However, most people believe that the ancestral spirits never kill their agnates. The ancestral spirit which is believed can kill, is that of the maternal grandmother or the spirit of *ngozi* (avenging spirit). Hence the Shona saying, *Mudzimu hauvurayi, unongorwadza chete* (The paternal ancestral spirit does not kill, it only torments).

As we have noted all along, the ancestral spirits are concerned with family issues. They are concerned with the welfare of their agnates. However, there are other spirits, tribal spirits, which are concerned with the problems which affect the tribe as a whole. Such problems are that of drought, death of livestock or any other misfortunes that affect the whole tribe. Let us now turn to these tribal spirits (*masvikiro*).

3.4 The tribal spirits

The tribal spirits occupy a higher hierarchy than the family ancestral spirits in the Shona belief system. These spirits are concerned with tribal matters. They are the ones who become offended when people till the land on *chisi* (a day set aside for rest in honour of the tribal spirits).

Gelfand (1982) notes that a person who is chosen by the spirits to be a medium, first becomes ill before he/she can be a medium. The *n'anga* (diviner) informs the relatives of the ill person that the tribal spirits wants to possess the ill person. The relatives brew beer and perform a ceremony on which the spirit is received. At such a ceremony, there is beating of drums or playing of rattles depending on the cultural group which performs the ritual.

At the ceremony, there will be other spirit mediums who lead the function. When the person is possessed he/she is asked questions about the tribe/clan's genealogy to prove that he/she is actually possessed. Knowledge of the clan will be proof enough for the person to be accepted as possessed with the tribal spirit. From there onwards, the medium is consulted on tribal issues.

When there is a problem say of drought, such spirit medium is approached by the elders and make their grievances known. The spirit medium can explain where people erred and tell them to make amend so that there will be rainfall. Livestock deaths or destruction of crops by the pests (locust or birds) are taken as punishment from tribal spirits. The spirits are consulted to find out what went wrong.

The Shona people believe that the tribal spirits can withhold rainfall if people do not brew beer or revere these spirits. One character, Nyanguru, in a play written by Mashiri (1987) titled *Ushe Ndehwangu* says,

> Nhamo yedu munyika muno ndeyekuti hatisisina she anobika doro
>
> remukwerera! Hatisisina she anopira midzimu yedu! Mvura inganaya
>
> sei kana isingateurwi! (9-10)
>
> (Our problem in this area is that we no longer have a chief who brews
>
> beer for rain making ceremony! We do not have a chief who prays to our
>
> ancestors! How can the rain fall if we do not worship the ancestors?).

The spirit medium is also consulted in the succession of chiefs. The medium is the one which names the successor after the death of a chief. This is so because the medium is believed to know the genealogy of a particular tribe.

Finally Shona religion cannot be complete without other two belief systems namely the *uroyi* (witchcraft) and *ngozi* (avenging spirit) beliefs. We start by interrogating *muroyi/uroyi* (witch/witchcraft) beliefs and then the *ngozi* (avenging spirit) belief.

3.5 Belief in *uroyi* (witchcraft)

The Shona people have a strong belief in witchcraft. The 1898 Witchcraft Suppression Act which tried to eradicate the belief in witchcraft by punishing people who accuse others of being witches has no significant impact to the belief in witchcraft. Zvarevashe (1970:48) defines a *muroyi* (witch) by noting,

> The Shona word *muroyi* (plural *varoyi*) means a 'witch' and
> nearly always refers to a woman. A woman travels at night
> visiting those places and people she wants to harm.

However, Tatira (1989) and Chavhunduka (1994) contend that the word *muroyi* (witch), is a fluid term and is difficult to define. A hard hearted, introvert person can be called *muroyi* (witch). However, when we apply the term *muroyi* (witch) in its primary meaning, we refer to those people who harm others through their magical powers be they man or woman.

There are two broad categories of *varoyi* (witches) which are *varoyi vamasikati* (day witches) and *varoyi veusiku* (night witches). Most often than not, *varoyi veusiku* are women and use familiars and *varoyi vamasikati* are usually men and they use no familiars.

3.5.1 *Varoyi veusiku* (night witches)

The Shona believe that these witches operate under the cover of darkness. They use familiars to assist them in their nocturnal visits. Witches rub a white substance so that they become invisible as they move from village to village.

If a witch is married, it is believed that she bewitches her husband so that he never wakes up in her absence. Some believe that the witch puts a dog in the bed to replace her as she goes out to bewitch. Some witches are believed to operate in groups with a leader giving them assignments. Each night they meet under a big tree to strategise the episode of the day. During the night, they harm and cause their victims to be ill. If not treated by a *n'anga* (diviner) these victims may die.

It is believed that when a witch arrives at a victim's home, she pleads with the victim's ancestral spirits to allow her in. The ancestors become flattered or are convinced that they should open and thus open the door to the witch. After bewitching her victims, she asks the ancestors to close the door and she departs. There is another belief which says the witch mysteriously opens the door and closes the door through her mystical magical powers without appealing to the victim's ancestral spirits.

3.5.2 Familiars

The witch must have familiars which help her in the operation of her duties. Such familiars can be hyenas, snakes, owls, ghosts and *hurekure* (marshy bird). The hyena is used as a mode of transport during the night visits while the *hurekure* (marshy bird) is believed to lead the hyena. The snakes, owls and ghosts are normally sent to carry out assignments on behalf of the witch.

On the use of familiars, Tatira (1989:34) observes,

> A *muroyi* uses these familiars or any one of them for reasons
>
> that he/she might be lazy to operate or is too busy operating
>
> elsewhere or is incapacitated by the situation to carry out the proposed venture.
>
> Snakes are used during the day or by the night. The witch instructs them as one
>
> would instruct a child when sending him to do something.

The *muroyi* (witch) and her familiars are believed to be able to cause illness. The illness caused by the familiars will subsequently lead to death if the sick person is not treated. If the victim dies, it is believed that witches visit the grave at night and feed upon the flesh of the deceased. The witches are believed to have a sharp appetite for human flesh. Generally traditional Shona people believe that illness is mostly caused by witches.

If there is always illness in the family, it should be explained in terms of witchcraft. If so many people die of the same disease in a community, the explanation may be that there is a witch who is causing such deaths. In such circumstances, the community usually resorts to *gumbwa* (divination performed to find out who are the witches in a community).

However the belief in witchcraft as Bourdillon (1982:165) notes,

> …does not necessarily contradict belief in natural causes…
> invisible causes are sought to explain sickness only when
> causes appear inadequate.

It is only after the sickness fails to go that the Shona suspect that the sickness should have been caused by witchcraft. Tatira (1989:27) shares the same opinion when he writes about the Karanga, a subgroup of the Shona. He says,

> …to the Karanga people, sickness is natural. But it ceases to be
> natural when it threatens life or when it lingers for too long
> without healing. When illness threatens life it becomes no longer
> natural, therefore the Karanga people go to the diviner. This diviner
> is believed not only to prescribe medicine for healing the sick but most
> often unveils the cause of illness.

Therefore, the Shona people are capable of separating the natural illness from the unnatural. They do not go to a diviner just because one has fallen ill. They appeal to their life experience about diseases before they consult a diviner.

3.5.3 *Varoyi vemasikati* (Day witches)

These witches are mostly men who employ black magic to harm others (Zvarevashe, 1970). These witches do not have familiars. They can use their black medicine to poison others by using *muchetura* (poison). *Muchetura* (poison) can be laced on the food or put in the drink the victim is supposed to take. *Chitsinga* (black medicine used to harm a person). *Chitsinga* can cause one to be crippled or have a swollen leg depending on the type of *chitsinga*.

Varoyi vemasikati (day witches) usually use their witchcraft to harm their adversaries, usually at work- places. At work- place they use *chitsinga* but when *chitsinga* is used at work place, it is normally called *muposo* hence *wakaposiwa* (he/she was bewitched at work- place). The victim of *muposo*, can lose sight when he/she gets in the office to do business. If he/she is a driver he/she can fail to see the road. There are stories of such victims seeing a pool each time they want to drive. If such victims are not at work, they are said to be normal. The problem only emanates when they go to work. There are different types of *muposo* which cannot all cannot be given in this book.

3.5.4 How does one become a *muroyi* (witch)?

Finally let us see briefly how one becomes a *muroyi* (witch). There are several ways of becoming a *muroyi* (witch). *Uroyi* (witchcraft) can be inherited from a dead grandmother, normally a maternal grandmother. The person can become ill and the diviner tells her that a bewitching spirit of a relative wants to use her. A ritual can be performed to accept the spirit.

The other type of witchcraft is that of the maternal grandmother or rarely paternal grandmother gives the grandchild witchcraft. This is done by incising, then rubbing the medicine in the body of the recipient. This is called *uroyi rwenhemerwa* (withcraft begotten though incision). This type of witchcraft can be received from the grandmother through the consent of the grandchild or when the grandchild will be in her sleep thus without her consent.

There is also *uroyi hweshavi* (witchcraft inherited from an alien spirit). This type of witchcraft comes as a result of a bewitching alien spirit (*shavi rekuroya*), which chooses a person as its medium. The spirit will be of a dead witch which enters into a person who is not related to it. The person can become ill and through divination one is told the cause of illness. Beer is brewed to accept the bewitching spirit. If one does not like the spirit, one can be exorcised by a traditional healer.

3.6 Belief in *ngozi* (avenging spirit)

The *ngozi* (avenging spirit) belief among the Shona is a complex belief system. This belief holds that once one kills a person, the spirit of the killed person will fight back. The Shona people are more afraid of *ngozi* (avenging spirit) rather than the criminal element of killing. Gombe (1986:132) has an elaborate description of *ngozi* (avenging spirit). He describes it in the following words,

Ngozi mweya wemunhu akafa nefiro isina kururama kana kuti
akafa nokupondwa zvemaune munhu aine chinangwa chekuuraya.
Mweya uyu unozodzoka kuvanhu vemhuri yakapfudza upenyu
hwawo uchibvunza mhosva yawo. Unokonzera minyama yakawanda
nendufu dzakawanda dzinogona kuuya nenzira dzakasiyana-siyana uye
dzinonetsa kunzwisisa.

(Avenging spirit is the spirit of the deceased person who was killed through
violence or other means, not by accident but purposely. This spirit comes back
to the family of its killers asking why they killed him/her. This spirit causes
numerous misfortunes and deaths which are difficult to understand).

The Shona people believe that normally the killed person's spirit comes back soon after
the body has decomposed (*munhu aputika*). The spirit fights back by causing death to the
family killer. Members of the killer's family die frequently in an unnatural way. The
family misfortune can be the talk of the community. Members of the family of the killer
can become mad. While possessed, they can for, example, say, "Why did you kill me?".
It is normal for the family members of the killer to consult a traditional healer, who
would advise them to appease the spirit by paying a fine to the deceased person's
relatives. They are usually told to pay a large number of cattle as compensation. In
some cases, they are asked to give a member of their family to the killed person's family
as compensation.

The spirit of the killed person is generally believed to fight back without having been
invoked by the relatives. However, in some cases, the relatives of the deceased person
are the ones who invoke the spirit to fight back (*kumutsa ngozi*). This happens when the
relatives are not sure of the cause of the death but suspect foul play. The relatives can
go to a traditional healer and are given medicine. They mix such medicine with water in
a calabash. The calabash with this medicine is crushed on top of the grave. The person
will invoke the deceased's spirit to fight back. The person will leave the grave crying
loudly to express his/her grieve.

It is believed that the deceased's spirit will fight the killer's family until it is fully compensated. Others invoke the spirit to fight back by beating the grave with a *shamhu* (a flexible stick) soon after burial. The relative will invoke the deceased not to remain in the grave but to go and fight its killers.

Finally Shona people believe that there is no remedy for avenging spirit other than compensating the family of the killed person hence they say, *mushonga wengozi kuiripa* (the only remedy to *ngozi* is to pay the required fine).

3.7 Change in the belief system among the Shona people

The missionaries came to Zimbabwe with a religion which emphasised the belief in God without intermediaries of ancestors. This means that some Shona people who were converted to the Christian faith are no longer practicing ancestral worship. There is another group, which did not accept Christian faith but still are skeptical about ancestral worship. This group practice neither Christian faith nor ancestral worship. Still there is another group which practice Christianity but at the same time remains in ancestral worship. This group has it both ways Christianity and traditional religion.

The beliefs in *n'anga*, *ngozi* and *uroyi* have also been affected by Christianity. Some people have turned to Christianity when afflicted by *ngozi* and believe that the blood of Jesus Christ has power over all evil spirits. They do not consult a *n'anga* and no longer believe in the effects of *uroyi*.

Still quite a large number of Shona people firmly believe in *ngozi*, *uroyi* and *n'anga*. The belief in *midzimu*, *varoyi*, *ngozi* and *n'anga* among the Shona people, is very prevalent. Though we do not have stastical evidence to back the claim, we are still convinced that a large percentage of the Shona people are still engrossed in these beliefs.

3.8 Summary

In summary, the following points are of particular importance,

- That the Shona people have their belief system like any other people on earth. This belief system helps the Shona to rationalise their misfortunes as well as successes.

- The Shona have a concept of God and they are monotheistic in their approach to their religion.

- They have various names which they use to refer to God and the names they use have attributes to God as creator of all things, the all powerful, giver of blessings etc.

- The Shona's concept of God is that He is very senior and that He should not be contacted directly but through ancestral spirits.

- The Shona people believe in *varoyi* (witches) and *ngozi* (avenging spirit).

- There are two categories of *varoyi* (witches) which are *varoyi vemasikati* (day witches) and *varoyi veusiku* (night witches).

- Some *varoyi* (witches) use familiars while others do not.

- *Uroyi* (witchcraft) can be acquired consciously or unconsciously.

- Finally, though the Shona belief system has been affected by Christianity, the belief system remains quite strong among the Shona people.

Chapter 4

4.0 The Rites of Passage

4.1 Introduction

In the Shona society, birth, death and burial are memorable occasions in the life cycle of a Shona person. The birth of a Shona child is accompanied by pomp and fanfare. It is time for celebration and thanking the ancestral spirits for a new life brought on earth. Death is shrouded by misery, and suspicion. This is the occasion of sorrow and reflection. The Shona people reflect on what might have gone wrong, what might have disappointed the ancestral spirits that they did not protect the deceased against the misfortune of death.

The rituals performed after burial are performed in order to bring society in terms with reality. The mourning period should end and people should make positive arrangements to see that despite the misfortune, life should continue. A new lease of vigour should be blown into the surviving members. The way forward is planned and executed. People are given roles to see that life still continues. The aspirations of the dead are carried forward by the close relatives.

Some of the rituals and things done on the birth of a child, the burial of a person and subsequent ceremonies have changed with time. New things have been introduced in some of the stages or old things modified. However some of the rituals are still carried as they used to be in the olden days of the Shona people despite the influence of Christianity and western values. In the sections which follow, we would like to investigate the beliefs associated with birth, death and burial.

4.2 Beliefs associated with Birth, Death and Burial

4.2.1 Birth

Just before the birth of the first child, there are some rituals which the Shona people do to ensure that the pregnant person delivers well. Traditionally the son-in-law was supposed to hand back his wife to her parents a few months before birth. This was only done for the first pregnancy. The wife was brought back to her family for some of the following reasons:

i. So that the mother-in-law could give her daughter some medicine. The medicine was believed to enable the wife to deliver without problems,

ii. The practice was also associated with the ancestral spiritual beliefs. The Shona people believe that the mother-in-law could better communicate with her ancestors if there was a problem related to the pregnancy. It is believed that the ancestors that are responsible for fertility are the mother-in-law's ancestors, therefore she can best plead with them if there is any problem.

iii. The practice was done so as to afford the pregnant woman enough time to rest and relax. It is a well known fact that long back daughters-in-law stayed in their mother-in-law's compound until the birth of the first child. It was normally after they delivered the first child, that there were free to move to their separate hut. In such circumstances it could have meant that the daughter-in-law could have forced herself to work in the fields or at home to prove that she was a good daughter-in-law, even though she might have felt that she needed to rest. Therefore, going back to her home where there were no *vanyarikani* (people who one is not free to be himself/herself) gave her ample opportunity to rest.

iv. The first pregnancy can be traumatic. Emotions can be negatively affected, the eating patterns and appetite can change. The pregnant woman should necessarily be with people she can easily confide to. She must be able to freely ask questions, some of the questions which might need a very close person like one's mother.

v. The woman's mother might have experienced similar problems when she had her first pregnancy hence can offer ready answers and solutions to problems.

4.2.2 *Kusungira* (The process of handing over the wife to the in-law for the birth of the first child)

The son-in-law was supposed to go to his in-laws with a he-goat. He goes in the company of elderly relatives together with the *munyai* (intermediary). The practice could vary from place to place. The goat would be shown to the father-in-law who would instruct the son-in-law to slaughter it. Some of the goat's meat is mixed with medicine which is given to the daughter to eat. Gelfand (1977:50) explains,

> The father-in-law adds some medicine… Before they start,

the father takes a piece of stiff porridge (musuwa), dips it

into the gravy and gives it to his daughter to eat. After this

the rest of people begin their meal. This concludes the ceremony.

It should be noted that the intermediary was given part of the meat, normally the whole shoulder blade. Long back the son-in-law could remain with his in-laws for some few days helping the in-laws with his labour.

4.2.3 *Kupereka* (Going back with the new born baby to its paternal family)

Normally word was sent to the baby's paternal family through an intermediary to inform them that there was a baby. Close relatives, from the man's family would go to see the baby but they did not take the baby. It was the duty of the wife's family to bring the baby to its paternal home.

The mother of the newly born child was supposed to stay for a while before she joined her husband's family. This was done to allow her to recuperate from the pains associated with pregnancy and birth. Close relatives of the woman such as *vatete* (aunt), *mainini* (sister to the mother) and *mbuya* (wife to the mother's brother) would normally accompany the woman and her baby to her husband's place.

The delegation was supposed to be given money as a token for them to enter into the yard of the in-laws. They were again supposed to be paid money to show the in-laws the baby. After these procedures celebrations started. The following day, the close relatives who accompanied the woman will prepare food for the whole family. They prepare *sadza* (stiff porridge) from *mapfunde* (sorghum) or *rukweza* (finger millet) or *mupunga* (rice). This is served with chicken. All the things which are prepared would have been bought from the woman's family. People eat and the celebration continues for the whole day. Masasire (1996:47) on the same subject notes, "The mother's reincorporation into the group is usually marked by a feast"

On the following day these close relatives go back to their respective homes except *vatete* (sister to the wife's father). She remains behind for two or so days. Her duty was to see that the new mother can handle and feed the baby well. The husband is also required to provide a goat which is slaughtered. The slaughtered goat is meant for the wife so that good nutrition for. This goat in other places is known as *mbudzi yemafundo* (the goat meant to be eaten by breast feeding wife).

4.3 Why Kupereka?(Going back with the new born baby to its paternal family)

There are reasons why the Shona people make an elaborate procedure when they bring the woman with a new baby back to her husband. Some are the following reasons for this,

i. A woman who has given birth cannot be let to go back on her own to his husband's home as though she has no relatives.

ii. It is a way to celebrate a new life brought on earth by two families. This joint celebration is important to show that the child does not belong to one family but instead belongs to both families. The relationship is cemented by the birth of the child.

iii. The relatives from the father-in-law will be showing their in-laws what they expect them to give their daughter, that is , good diet, as exemplified by the food they bring with them, *rukweza* (finger millet), *huku* (chicken), *mupunga* (rice) and *mapfunde* (sorghum).

iv. Finally it can be said that it was a way of showing the man's family that the in-laws have given back the woman and baby in good health. If there was illness, it is discussed with the in-laws and solutions were taken on how to have either the baby or the wife treated.

4.4 The Practice today

These days there are a few people if any who follow the procedures in detail as outlined above when a child is born. The practice is still prevalent but some short cuts have been improvised here and there. The main reason why people cannot follow the procedures to the alphabet is because of the changing times.

Industrialisation has brought people further apart and the demands of the labour market have left people with little time to make elaborate procedures when a child is born. The constraints of time due to working schedules that we find in the urban areas have meant that, sometimes it is the mother-in-law who comes to stay with her daughter at the son-in-law's place before the daughter delivers. As a result the child is now born at its paternal family. The son-in-law in this case is the first to know that there is a baby rather than the in-laws informing him.

However, the procedure of bringing the wife back to her family, for the birth of the first child seems to be followed though in a modified way. The son-in -law can just go with a goat, spend a night with the in-laws and takes her wife with him the following morning to the urban area, where there are modern facilities. Other in-laws perform the *kusungira* ritual well after the child has been born. They will just go to the father -in-law with a goat and inform him the purpose of their visit and slaughter the goat after being instructed by the in-law to do so. After a meal with the father-in-law's family, they can return to their home. Others just leave the goat with the in-laws who will decide what to do with the goat. In other cases, the *kupereka* ritual is also performed well after the child has been born.

4.5 Death

After an individual is born, what is left is to exit the earth through death. Everyone human being knows very well that one day he/she will die but many people are not prepared to die. The traditional Shona person, mostly views death as primarily caused by evil spirits or witchcraft. A few people, if any accept death as a natural exit from the earth depending on the age of the person who died or how he died. The death of a very old person, in very few cases, is the one which can be considered as a natural death by some Shona people. Generally, the Shona people ask themselves why a particular person died and why on that particular day. These questions make it difficult for them to accept death as a natural exit from the earth. It is not easy to describe in detail what the Shona people do when a person dies because what they do vary from place to place. However what would be noted here will give the reader a fair picture of what is done. Now let us see what the Shona people do when a person dies.

4.6 *Kupeta mufi* (Attending to a person soon after death)

Soon after a person dies, those attending to him/her, usually elderly close relatives, that is if he/she dies at home, close the eyes and mouth. They will fold the hands and stretch the legs straight but close to each other. The head will be positioned so that the corpse faces upwards. The whole body will be like a person sleeping on his/her back facing upwards with hands stretched along the ribs. After this the body will be covered with a cloth or blanket. Another cloth/blanket will be veiled covering the corpse.

Soon after such an exercise, people will start *kuridza mhere* (to cry with a loud voice). Neighbours would arrive and the word of the death spreads like fire. In no time the homestead is filled with mourners.

However, even if the word reaches certain special or respected individuals, normally such individuals would not come to the funeral unless they are officially told of the death. Such individuals would be the man's in-laws if it is his wife who has died. The son-in-law is traditionally expected to send a person to go and inform the in-laws about the death of his wife. The sent person should carry with him the money to give the in-laws as a token to announce the death news. This money is called *mari yemhere* (a token to announce death news to the in-laws).

The other person who is supposed to be told about the death is a village head. The village head is not given money when informing him about the death. The village head should be informed because he is the custodian of the land on which the deceased would be buried. If the family has an unsettled case with the village head's court, the issue should be resolved first before the village head allows the deceased to be buried. The in-laws can also prevent the burial of their daughter if they feel that the son-in-law needs to finish payment of lobolo or if there are outstanding cases which need to be settled before burial.

If it is a man who has died, the procedure is the same on reporting of the death, only that the in-laws are not paid anything when relatives announce to their in-laws the death of the son-in-law.

4.7 Burial

Normally a person is not supposed to be buried the day he/she dies. This is done to allow relatives to travel to the deceased's place. A person is buried a day or so after his/her death. The time is provided such as to allow people to have enough time to prepare for the funeral and also to give dignity for the deceased. If the burial is hurried, it deprives people enough time to mourn the deceased person.

Before a person is buried, a corpse is washed and dressed in the best attire. The issue of who washes the body depends on the relationship involved and the practice of a particular people.

After the body has been washed and is ready for the burial, mourners or close relatives are asked to view the body before burial. Traditionally, the most senior member in the deceased's family addresses the ancestral spirits before the body is taken out for burial. Even these days, some people still address ancestral spirits before the body is taken for burial. They will address the ancestral spirits asking them to accompany the deceased to the unknown world as well as that they should facilitate the welcoming of the deceased by others who departed long back. Other people just have a word of prayer while yet others have both prayer and an address to the ancestors.

As to who are supposed to carry the corpse to the grave, this varies from place to place. In other places people like the deceased's children (if they are old enough), carry their father's body. The other people who can carry the body are the son-in-laws, uncles, friends or fellow church members. Normally, the body will be in a coffin. In other areas, the body is taken right round the homestead before it is taken to the grave. The rationale behind this practice varies from people to people. Some say that the deceased should be shown his/her homestead before burial. Others say that this is done in order to confuse the spirit so that it won't come back before *kurova guva* (a ceremony performed to bring back the spirit of the deceased).

Before the *kurova guva* (a ceremony performed to bring back the spirit of the deceased) ceremony is performed, the spirit of the deceased is believed to be dangerous, as we shall see later, hence is supposed to be kept away from the home.

People who carry the corpse to the grave put the coffin on the ground before they reach the grave, *kuzorodza mufi* (to allow the deceased to take a rest) and carry it again. The process can be repeated twice before they reach the grave. At the grave, it is the close relatives who go into the grave in order for them to lay the body in the grave. Before the body is laid in the grave, a reed mat is placed down first. The corpse/coffin is placed on top of the reed mat. Thereafter, the people who dug the grave can take over to finish the process.

A selected group of relatives are given time to speak about the deceased, his/ her illness, a bit of his/ her life history, his/her achievements and to any other things the speaker might want to say. Friends can also be given an opportunity to speak. In the rural areas, people like a chief, village head and a councilor are usually given an opportunity to speak. In most areas the village head announces days of rest in respect of the deceased. These days are called *mahakurimwi* (days in which the whole village should not work in respect of the deceased). At this point, those who owe the deceased are asked to say what they owe him/her as well as those who are owed by the deceased. After the speeches and filling up of the grave with earth, mourners normally wash hands and go back to the homestead to feed.

4.8 Ceremonies performed after burial

There are ceremonies which are performed after burial and these ceremonies depend on the age and whether the deceased is married or not. If a person is not an adult and not married, normally no ceremony is held after his/her death.

After the death of a person, the Shona as tradition dictates, they go to consult a diviner to find the cause of death. The visit to the diviner takes place some few days after the burial of the deceased. Relatives would normally like to know the cause of the death so that they would prevent other misfortune from befalling the family. Sometimes they would like to be given medicine to revenge the person who they think caused the death.

Sometimes the diviner can tell the deceased's relatives to brew beer to appease the ancestral spirits or do other rituals to make right the wrong they committed which they believe caused death. Such rituals would not be directly related to the deceased but are directed to protect the surviving family members.

When an adult married person dies, there is normally a ceremony marked by beer brewing. This ceremony normally takes place a month after burial. The ceremony is called *hwahwa rehonye* (beer brewed after peple think the corpse has just decomposed). Mandaza (1970:57) puts it at two weeks. He explains:

> In about two weeks's time, beer to mark the decay of
>
> the body (hwahwa hwehonye) is brewed ... at the home of
>
> the deceased man. This is a very simple ceremony and beer
>
> drinking and tribal dancing are important features.

In some areas, the same ceremony is called *doro remvura* and yet in other areas is called *doro remafoshora*. The occasion is meant to thank people who assisted in the burial of the deceased. People drink beer and eat goat meat in a more relaxed atmosphere because the funeral would be over.

It is only after a year or so after burial that a serious ceremony of *kurova guva* (ceremony of bringing back the spirit of the deceased) is performed. In the next subsection we will give in detail the *kurova guva* (the ceremony meant to bring back the spirit of the deceased).

4.9 *Kurova Guva /kugadzira* (the ceremony meant to bring back the spirit of the deceased)

Traditionally, Shona people believe that a person survives another life after this physical life. They, like Christians believe in the hereafter but they differ in their conception of the hereafter. The traditional Shona person believes that the deceased's spirit has influence over the lives of the living relatives especially his/her children. As a result, they perform a ritual to bring back the deceased's spirit to its family. On the hand, Christians believe that the deceased has no influence whatsoever to his family. Once dead, they believe that one goes to heaven or hell and to them this marks the end of history. To the traditional Shona people, it is not by any way an end of history but a beginning of yet another episode.

Before the *kurova guva* (the ceremony of bringing back the spirit of the deceased) is held, close relatives of the deceased have to seek the advice of a diviner if they can go ahead with the ceremony. The visit to the diviner is necessary so that if there is anything which might derail the ceremony, things are corrected before the ceremony flops. The manner in which the ceremony takes place varies from place to place. However, what is outlined below are the general things which take place at such ceremonies.

In most cases, people dance and sing throughout the night. During the day of this same night, a goat would have been dedicated to the ancestral spirit *mbudzi yemudzimu* (a goat set aside for the ancestral spirit). Water is poured on the back of the goat while the sister to the deceased or brother or father addresses it. The goat is called by the name of the deceased and is told that they are returning him back home. If the goat shakes its body, women ululate and men clasps hands and there is joy. The joy emanates from the belief that once the goat shakes its body, the deceased has accepted to be brought back and therefore the ceremony is going to be successful. The goat is slaughtered and all the meat is roasted. All the roasted meat is eaten without salt.

The following morning, very early in the morning, the gathering goes to the grave. They clasp their hands while a senior person addresses the grave (deceased's spirit), asking him/her how he/she has spent the night. One would thing he/she is addressing a living person. The senior person then informs the buried person that they are taking him/her back home to look after his/her family.

Beer is poured at the top of the grave, some leave the empty pot of beer there and take it after the ceremony while others go with the pot home. After this grave ritual, women ululate and men clasp hands. They then go back home singing traditional songs like *Mudzimu tauya nawo* (We have brought the ancestral spirit). At the homestead, a mat is spread and the eldest son sits on the mat and people address him in the deceased's name. This happens if the ceremony is that of a man. People tell the eldest son to look after the family. The son is presented with gifts by people present, *kupemberera mudzimu* (celebrating that the spirit of the deceased is back home) there will be ululation and clasping of hands.

Normally it is at this ceremony that the deceased's property is shared and the practice is called *kugova nhaka* (sharing of the deceased's property). Only things like clothes are shared among the relatives while the durables and the immovable are left for the deceased's dependents. Such property is managed by the eldest son with the help of his mother or his father's brothers. Traditionally, the wife of the deceased would also be inherited by either her husband's younger brother or in extreme cases by the son of her husband's sister. If the ceremony is for a woman, all what has been said to a man's ceremony is true to a woman's. The only difference comes at *kugova nhaka* (sharing of the deceased's property). At this ceremony, most if not all property like kitchen utensils go back to her original home. If she had cattle, they are taken back to her original home. The surviving husband can be given another wife by the in-laws.

4.10 Impact of foreign influence on the rites of passage among the Shona people

In the process of our discussion on birth and marriage, we have discussed the impact of urbanisation and Christianity on these institutions. Now we would also like to discuss how these impact on death, *kurova guva* (the ceremony meant to bring back the spirit of the deceased) and *nhaka* (sharing of the property of the deceased).

Urban life and Christianity have forced some of the practices to be abandoned while others have been modified to suit circumstances. In urban areas, people are buried on town council grounds which are bought for the purpose of burial. The chief and his traditional leaders fall away. The graves are dug by the city council workers and as a result the ceremony done after burial to thank people who assisted by digging the grave falls away. The *doro rehonye* we have discussed before falls away. Some Christians no longer perform the *kurova guva* ceremony. Some people have embraced Christianity but still feel that the ceremony is indispensible thus they continue with the practice. They still believe in ancestral practices. This is why other scholars of religion argue that you can never convert an African.

Christianity had a great impact on the practice of wife inheritance because of its emphasis on monogamy. Many Christians are not interested in inheriting a wife and therefore the practice is not so prevalent among the Christians. The modern economy has also rendered the practice redundant. People who live in urban areas find it impossible or difficult to accommodate two families in urban areas where there is no space to accommodate a large family. The economic resources which are scarce also make it difficult for a person to take another wife.

Apart from the above factors, women are now educated and most of them like to manage their own affairs after the death of their husbands. In the case were a woman is asked to marry the husband of her deceased sister or aunt, many woman now refuse. The practice has suffered a further blow because of the AIDS pandemic. People are afraid of getting into a union with a person who has lost a partner lest the person is suffering from AIDS.

In conclusion, it can be noted that while the burial and the ceremonies that follow in some cases remain being practiced, the idea of wife inheritance is fast losing currency. Western education, Christianity, urbanisation and the AIDS pandemic have greatly contributed to the demise of the practice.

4.11 Summary

The chapter has discussed important stages in the rites of passage which are summarised as follows,

- Birth, death and burial are important rites of passage in Shona people's lives.

- Birth is a celebrated occasion which cement the relationship of two families in Shona society.

- Before the birth of the first child the woman is normally handed back to her family. The family looks after the woman until the birth of a child.

- Nowadays, the mother-in-law can look after her daughter at her son-in-law's home' especially in urban areas.

- Some days after the birth, the woman and the baby are accompanied by their aunts to the woman's husband. A celebration to welcome the baby takes place. This practice is known as *kupereka.*

- Death is most often taken as caused by witchcraft and evil spirits among the Shona people.

- When a person dies, close relatives are informed as a matter of rule.

- Another person who is not a relative but who is expected to be informed is a village head that is when a person dies or is buried in the rural areas.

- Normally a person is buried a day or so after his/her death so as to allow relatives from afar to come for the ceremony.

- Close relatives are responsible for washing the body before burial.

- After burial, normally, if the deceased is a married adult, some ceremonies are performed.

Chapter 5

5.1 Revision questions
5.2 Introduction

This chapter is intended to guide readers by given them revision questions for each chapter covered in this book. These are essay questions and they are mere guides. It does not mean that questions given for each chapter are exhaustive.

5.3 Chapter 1

1) Account for the possible origin of the Shona people.

2) Make a critical appraisal of the conception of the Shona family.

3) Evaluate the impact of western religion and education on the Shona family.

5.4 Chapter 2

1) What is the Shona concept of marriage?

2) Describe any two obsolete ways of getting married and argue why they are no longer practiced.

3) State the advantages of any two ways of getting married.

4) 'Shona marriages last longer because they are not crafted by individuals'. Discuss.

5) 'Culture changes with time'. Evaluate this statement with reference to some ways of getting married.

5.5 Chapter 3

1) 'The Shona people are monotheistic'. Evaluate this statement.

2) 'The Shona people's world view is controlled by their ancestral spirits'. Discuss.

3) Explain in detail how a *muroyi* (witch operates).

4) Explain how a deceased person in Shona belief can fight back.

5) Discuss different Shona beliefs among the Shona.

5.6 Chapter 4

1) Explain what the traditional Shona people do just before the birth of a child and soon after the birth.

2) Advance a rationale for *kusungira* and *kupereka* among the Shona people.

3) Give a detailed appraisal of *kusungira* (the process of handing over the wife to the in-laws for the birth of the first child) and *kupereka* (going back with the new born baby to its paternal family) as they obtain today.

4) Explain what the traditional Shona people do from the time a person dies until he/she is buried.

5) Give a detailed description of a burial of an adult person in Shona society.

6) Why do the Shona people consider ceremonies they perform after the death of an adult important?

7) Pick at least two ceremonies performed by the Shona after the burial of the deceased showing how they have been affected by the modern world.

8) In your opinion why does the *kurova guva* (the ceremony of bringing back the spirit of the deceased) seem to stand the test of time?

Bibliography

Beach, D.N.   (1980) The Shona and Zimbabwe, Gweru, Mambo Press.

Bourdillon, M. F.   (1982) The Shona People, Gweru, Mambo Press.

Chigwedere, A.   (1980) From Mutapa to Rhodesia, Harare, MacMillan Publishers
                     Ltd.

Gelfand, M.   (1977) The Spiritual Beliefs of the Shona, Gweru, Mambo Press.

Gombe, J. M.   (1986) Tsika DzaVaShona, Harare, College Press.

Kahari, G.P.   (1975) The Novels of Patrick Chakaipa, Salisbury, Longman
                     Rhodesia.

Mandaza, D. M.   (1970) "Ceremonies which Persist" in Clive and Peggy Kileff (eds)
                     Shona Customs, Gweru, Mambo Press.

Masasire, A.   (1996) "Kinship and Marriage" in Mutswairo, S. M. et al,
                     Introduction to Shona Culture, Harare, Juta Zimbabwe
                     Pvt Limited, pp 40-49.

Mashiri, P.M.   (1978) Ushe Ndehwangu, Harare, Longman Rhodesia.

Masolo, D. A.   (1994) African Philosophy in Search of Identity, Nairobi, East Africa
                     Educational Publishers.

Mutswairo, S.M.   (1996) Introduction to Shona Culture, Harare, Juta Zimbabwe.

Nzita, R. and Niwampa, M. (1993) Peoples and Shona Cultures of Uganda, Kampala,
                     Fountain Publishing Ltd.

Radcliffe-Brown, R. A and Forde, D. (1950) African Systems of Kinship and Marriage,
                     London, Oxford University Press.

Seligman, C.G.   (1966) Races of Africa, London, Oxford University Press.

Tatira, L.   (1989) "The Muroyi and Uroyi beliefs among the Karanga People,"
                     Unpublished BA Honours Dissertation, Harare, University
                     of Zimbabwe.

Tatira, L.   (2000) <u>Zviera zvaVaShona</u>, Gweru, Mambo Press.

Tatira, L.   (2000b) "The role of zviera in socialization" in Chiome, E.M. et al,
                      <u>Knowledge and Technology in Africa and Diasporan</u>
                      <u>Communities: Multi-Disciplinary Approaches</u>,Harare,
                      U.S.A. National Council for Black Studies.

Weinrich, A. K. H.   (1982) <u>African Marriages in Zimbabwe and the Impact of</u>
                      <u>Christianity</u>, Gweru, Mambo Press.

Zvarevashe, I.M.   (1970) "Beliefs and Ritual" in Clive and Peggy Kileff (eds) <u>Shona</u>
                      <u>Customs</u>, Gweru, Mambo Press.

Lightning Source UK Ltd.
Milton Keynes UK
UKOW041936030413

208626UK00001B/37/P